CREATION

Accessing Your Untapped Potential

Purposeful Mind Series – Book One

Other Books by Helena Kalivoda

AWAKEN!
Your Soul Is Calling

WAKE UP!
Your Heart Is Calling

WAKE UP!
Prosperity Is Calling

Purposeful Mind Series:

CREATION
Accessing Your Untapped Potential

ILLUMINATION
Getting to Know the Invisible You

CONTEMPLATION
Understanding Your Inner World

EVOLUTION
It Is Time for the New You

METAMORPHOSIS
What Else Is Possible?

"An absolutely delightful collection of poetry that makes you stop and think, 'Am I approaching life in the way that best serves me?'. Helena's poetry is beautiful encouragement to live consciously."

—Tina Thrussell, speaker, author, facilitator, and coach

"Every single poem in CREATION spoke to me! *Deliberately Create Your Life, You Are the Centre of the Universe, Accommodate Yourself,* all of the *Change* chapter, *Clarity* chapter—I could go on and on, throughout the remainder of the book! It is really hard to pick out just one or two best liked in this volume! It was all wonderful to my ears and heart. If you are yearning for self-discovery and understanding your power give yourself the gift of reading this book."

—Sally Parsons, Reiki Master, EFT Practitioner, Artist, facilitator, speaker, teacher

"I loved CREATION! The messages of the book so resonated with me. Helena's poems spoke to me on many levels. They were exactly what I needed to hear. They assisted me in moments of uncertainty and doubt and in times of struggle. Her words helped me to understand why life is the way it is. I see now that life is a direct result of my own beliefs, thoughts and actions."

—John Beed, Artist

CREATION

Accessing Your Untapped Potential

Purposeful Mind Series – Book One

HELENA KALIVODA

AUDRENAR BOOKS

CREATION
Accessing Your Untapped Potential
Purposeful Mind Series – Book One

Copyright ©2012 by Helena Kalivoda
Published by Audrenar Books

Library and Archives Canada Cataloguing in Publication

Kalivoda, Helena,
Creation / Helena Kalivoda.

Poems.
ISBN 978-0-9877521-0-9

I. Title.

PS8621.A469C74 2012 C811'.6 C2012-902414-7

Editing: Agnes L. Kirby
Cover art: original oil painting by Jaroslav Kalivoda

For more information on this book and other books by Helena Kalivoda visit www.awakenbyhelena.ca.

*I am dedicating this series to my family
and to all who are searching to reconnect
with that part of divinity we call Self.*

CONTENTS

CLARITY

INTUITION

ABUNDANCE

ACKNOWLEDGEMENT

I am extending a heartfelt thank-you to my family for supporting me in my writing. My further thank-you goes to Agnes L. Kirby for her undivided attention when editing my manuscript. I am grateful to my husband for contributing his paintings of trees for the book covers of this series. Lastly, I am appreciative of all the help I received from my incarnate and spirit muses. Thank you all for your presence in my life.

Helena Kalivoda

PREFACE

Creation is the first of five books in the *Purposeful Mind* series. It is a poetic study of how to create your ideal self and reach your potential.

The topics in this book address many aspects of the human experience: conscious creation, intuition, imagination, clarity, abundance, the power to change from within, and more. Our primary responsibility to ourselves is to understand our role as the creator of our lives and become conscious in our creating, as, whether we are aware of it or not, we create. And what is the better way of living—creating consciously or being unconscious of our powerful self, expecting others to fulfill our destiny?

The ageless wisdom presented in these verses was transmitted to me from the realms of higher consciousness during the period of my life when I needed most to hear the truth of who we truly are: we are spiritual beings cloaked in our physical attire, living on our beautiful planet Earth.

When reading this book, allow yourself to be drawn into the rhythm of the verses. Read and listen to them through your heart. They will activate your mind and assist you in remembering your origins.

Helena Kalivoda

YOU AS A CREATOR

DELIBERATELY CREATE YOUR LIFE

Have it your way,
as that is always the best,
as you are on your quest,
as you are your own boss,
as there is no one else who drives you.

Abracadabra it ain't,
it is you who is splashing the paint,
splashing the paint on the canvas of your life.
Deliberately or not,
consciously or unconsciously,
it is always you.

Deliberately is a better option,
as then you know that you are in charge,
then you know that you are the boss.
From now on, be deliberate
in the ways you live your life.

Take heed today, be deliberate in your action.
Be your own osmosis.
Be your own deliberate teacher.
Live what you preach and teach by example.

Deliberately direct your inner powers
that will create the way
the world is formed around you.
Your inner power that creates your reality,
that comes from the inner strength,
that comes from the inner life,
that then shows outwardly,

that glows as a lighthouse
that is showing you the way as it intended to,
through you allowing yourself to create
deliberately.

Deliberately!
Deliberately is the way to create your way,
that may, and I am saying only may,
may appear as being something from outside
influencing you, being apart from you.
But that it is not, it is not.

You don't need to be a Saint to create your reality.
Reality is your invention, reality is yours, yours.
Anything that happens to you,
happens as you intended it to.

Just remember that,
and deliberately create your life.

WHAT YOU SEED IS WHAT YOU HARVEST

Beliefs are shattered and established.
Establish a belief that you are powerful
and you will be,
as this is what gets ingrained in you
and it will also be ingrained
in the people around you.

Think powerful and you will be.
You are a creator.
You are your reality maker.
Anything you want to be, think.

Would you like to be a writer?
Think you are.
Would you like to be a singer?
Think you are.
Would you like to be a mechanic?
Think you are.
And so on.

A deltoid grows if you exercise it.
Memory grows if you exercise it.
Intent grows if you exercise it.
All is repetitive thinking,
and then all is ingrained and working.
All, all, all.

Are you sad?
Sad things happen to you.
Are you mad?
Maddening is your life.

Are you sweet?
Sweet people will embrace you,
and so on.

The lesson is,
what you seed is what you harvest.
Que sera, sera? Oh, not so.
You are making the waves
that propel you toward the targets
and objects of your life.

BOSSED AROUND BY YOUR THOUGHTS?

Melancholy is of negative value.
What is the remedy?
Eat some dulse powder
and... no, just kidding.

Better approach is to understand the philosophy
based on positive thinking—
positive thoughts create positive reality.
Understand that reality that is seeded
from negative thoughts
is created because it is "needed"
by those who harbour negative thoughts.

A vicious circle encircles all
who are not in the atoll of happiness,
who feed on a field
of insincerity and despondency,
who are declaring the truth about the world
that is not a true image,
as they create, yet believe
it was bestowed unto them.

They continue in what they create further,
as they do not understand
that they are creators.
They can be damaging to all
and become carriers of disease.
They are not welcome in higher spheres,
as their thoughts are undermining
the structure of the Universes.

They say, oh well, what nonsense,
what a rudimentary mistake.
But, if you love yourself and understand,
then you will not, and we repeat,
you will not support such a plot
of negative thinking.

Heed this advice and break away
from feeding unhappiness,
as you contribute to your own demise.
For every negative thought,
have five happy thoughts
and that will teach you to become
more conscious of what you think.

You are an endless study of yourself.
You are your own example.
You are in a life drama that is so close to you.
You are ready to fight for your ideas,
and you don't see that you are actually
bossed around by your own thoughts.

YOU ARE THE CENTRE OF THE UNIVERSE

You create thought and thought creates you.
You are a creator of thought
and that thought influences you,
and so on.
Is this clear to you?

If not, let's see what else we can throw in.
Let's say the night is setting in.
The day is over and dark is spreading.
All of a sudden,
the wind rushes through the leaves
and the leaves start to shimmer in the wind.

The wind continues
and the leaves shimmer more
until the wind is a shimmer
and the leaves are the wind.

No? Not a very good example?
How about this?

You create a thought.
This thought follows its own path.
This thought is of a matter
that has not yet been solidified.

The thoughts of a similar nature
conglomerate together
until they are visually available,
and presto, reality comes to fruition,
it comes to be.

An avalanche of thoughts
is gathering speed to meet similar thoughts.
Once the mass is amassed,
the thoughts gel and become living reality.

The creator, you, may not like it.
But if she knew that she created it,
she may start thinking better thoughts
that will not take her on a path of destruction,
but on a path of self-realization.

Behold this fact—creation of the fields
is influenced by your thoughts.
Therefore you can say that the centre of you
is the centre of Universe.
And that is the truth.

YOU ALL CREATE MASS

Sometimes your own reality,
as it may seem to you,
is not what you want.
Why do you feel like it?
Well, because you have not made your bed
the way you want to sleep in it.

Be prepared to endure the hardship
if that is what you send yourself.
Be prepared to receive fruits and flowers
if that is what you send your way.

You choose probability
and then it becomes reality.
You choose every day and it is influenced
by not only what you choose,
but it is influenced by an ooze,
an ooze from other parties.
You, with others, create mass
that shifts from the intangible to real life.

YOU CAN BE AND DO ANYTHING

Worries are useless. Worries are taxing.
Worries are unbecoming, so why,
why all this waxing,
waxing over all that happens every day?

Don't you know that it is better
not to be so involved with all,
all that is so elusive and precarious,
as it is only a chimera of yours,
a chimera created by you,
a chimera, which is crawling
through your worlds?

It catches those who fear,
so much fear,
past, present and future,
who are full of worry every day.
Who are worried and anxious about
what will happen the next day.

Wake up! You are a creator.
Wake up! You are the one.
Listen and listen again,
please stop playing this game
of worry, of one who suffers and is so busy.

Be pleased with what you do.
Be thankful for your enchanted life.
Be your own guide.
Be your own decision maker.

Be the dutiful caretaker
of your own body and soul.
Be your own best friend.

What does it really mean? Well,
you will take care that you are kind to you.
You will not blame you.
You will not hurry you.
You will not sleep little.
You will not waste your time on the stuff
that does not matter.

You will not eat the food
that is not good for you.
You will not sulk, you will smile.
You will not pretend that you are a mile,
a mile away from eternal bliss,
as you can have all that you want,
as you can do, and this is not a plot,
you can do anything.

Remember, you are your own boss.
Remember, you are the maker
of your own Universe.
The choices are yours
and they always were yours.

You are a chooser, a reality maker.
You are the one
who creates your own reality
that is yours to behold and cherish.
It is yours, always was and will be.

WHAT YOU ASK FOR WILL COME TO YOU

Stifle your lower thoughts,
such as worries, fears and excuses.
Be clear, clean and transparent,
be fire and water,
be earth and wind.

Cry, and let go whenever you need.
Smile and laugh whenever you need.
As you need, you do.

As the water which falls from the sky,
as the wind that whistles through the trees,
as you do, you will receive relief.

Relief from the need and want.
Relief from the scourge of humanity
that is called fear and uncertainty.

Mais oui, mais oui, the sky is blue.
Mais oui, mais oui, it is true
that you are what you are.

You are a song that is free.
You are a smile that is free.
You are a cry that is free.

All is free, if you say so.
All is free, if you think so.
Not only a cry, a smile and a laugh,
you can have anything you ask.

What you ask for will come to you.
If you believe it, it will become true.
Mais oui, mais oui.

BE YOUR OWN GUEST

Be your own guest. Visit with yourself,
do not procrastinate anymore.
Take that plunge and you will be surprised
how it feels to be on your own.

Take a plunge into the unknown
to discover what you already have known.
Take a plunge and will yourself a destiny
that is more suited to your own scripting,
that is in line with your origins.

Meditate, and discover who you are.
Meditate, and be who you are—
yourself, yourself, yourself.
Yourself, the creator,
the manipulator of her own destiny.

Acquire endless bliss through knowing yourself.
Acquire understanding
through your full immersion
into your Soul Being.

ACCOMMODATE YOURSELF

Accommodate yourself into your schedule.
Your schedule is for you
and not for the others.

And even if you are taking care
of your sisters and brothers,
your time is your time,
your life is your life,
your apprenticeship is your apprenticeship,
and your accolades are yours to have.

Be with yourself and for yourself.
Be actively seeking yourself
in this maze of beings,
as you are your own solace and support,
and you are your own,
your very own guide.

Depending on yourself
your life is great or not so great.
You win, if you can accommodate yourself
with the ways of life that is yours,
only yours.

Your life is a life to be lived by you.
Your life can be a life that feels unfair to you,
if you don't understand
that the life you want to live
has to be made by you.

It must be made by you
by optimally selecting the thoughts
you send to yourself and others,
and by optimally saying, oh well,
I am not one to dwell on uncertainties,
I am aware of myself, of my wants and needs.

And then when I know,
I can be testing new grounds.
I can be opening new venues.
I can be literally moving mountains.
I can be calling the gods for help
and expecting them to come.

The lesson is, listen within and follow up,
and then the gods will help and will seek you out
to enable your truth and your wants.

ALIGN YOUR THOUGHTS WITH GOD'S

Remember, you are a creator,
you are responsible for your deeds.
You are responsible
for creating the ways you live.
You are responsible for absolute results,
your introduction to God,
and finishing your journey on Earth.

You cannot ask "them" to fix it.
You can only ask yourself to adapt
to the new and different thoughts
and send out thought signals
that herald the change,
that anticipate the better results,
and then better providence.

Providence shall take care of you
when your thoughts are aligned with God's.
Your neglect of that can lead
to the dismembering of your thought
from collective wisdom
that is the source of all inventions,
that is the source for inspiration,
and is the source of all new and old.

BE YOUR OWN GUIDE AND GUARDIAN

Presumably, all was said.
Presumably, all is done.
Now you can list your questions,
now you can find what you want.
Now you can eliminate things
that bother you.

You are changing to become a new person
who is welcome to visit, to peruse,
to applause, to question,
to murmur, to whisper—oh yes,
your whispers will also be heard
—to deliver all the worries,
all the requirements,
all sensible and foolish issues;
to deliver details, as many, as you need.

You can, and you will,
when you will have a good will.
Remember that you are a creator
and your own guide.
Appoint yourself your guardian
from now on, as you are the best one
to understand your own needs.

As your own guardian,
you can be intently watching you.
You can be intently searching for the clues
of your own wisdom, your own unhappiness,
your own lethargy or speediness.

YOU WILL AWAKEN AT FIRST SLOWLY

Cry, laugh, be merry.
Be your own decision maker.
Applaud your searching nature.
Applaud your second nature
that is first, but forgotten.

Your spirit is so overwhelming,
it is so prevalent
but when you are in a body
that is an equivalent
of the Spirit's home,
of the Spirit's welcomed safekeeping,
then you feel secure and warm,
you feel comfortable,
but—you are unaware.

Once you wake up and remember,
your body may feel like a prison
that is confining,
and you will not understand the reason
why you are in it at all.

You will awaken first slowly,
then faster and faster,
as you are working to become the master,
the master of your destiny.

Of your destiny,
of getting your freedom back,
of getting away from anything
that is dark, that is not light,

to that which is bright
and is shining on all
that you do and see.

WHAT IS IT GOING TO BE?

Cuckoo lays eggs
in someone else's nest.
Cuckoo is curious
of what is hatching right and left
and itself is unaware
what is in her own, very own nest.

Being unaware
is like being wrapped in a cocoon
that is windowless and dark,
that is confining and stark,
that has many layers,
and it takes so long
to unwrap those long, long folds
of fine film wrapper
that is called the physical Universe.

Who is the first in your life? It is you.
Who is your leader? It is you.
Who is your teacher? It is you.
You are all that is important.
You are all that is precious.
You are all that you need,
and no greed for other things
can add any value to it.

You are a spiritual being.
You are the center of your Universe.
You are the mother of your thought
that is powerful and creates a new world.

So, what is it going to be?
Don't be a cuckoo who lays eggs
in someone else's nest,
and then cannot see the fruition
of her own creation.

CHANGE

YOU, THE CREATOR, SET THE STAGE

Time is measured in hours, minutes and seconds.
Time is measured in days, weeks and years.
All this adds up to space in the Universe
then it is listed as change,
as in autumn to winter, young to old.

Change itself can be sudden.
Change can be perceived or not.
Change is a way of saying
I will not stay where I am,
I want to create something new
that I will enjoy any way it comes my way.

And then, oops, it is not enjoyed,
as change brings new realities,
and change brings new challenges
that have not been perceived.

Change changes you, and those and these.
Then you look for the main creator
of your unease, but the creator is you.

How do you decide what you need to change?
Do you need to change yourself or circumstances?
Do you need to change yourself or others?
Do you need to change your habit of making
changes?

Or do you need to change at all?

You decide, as you, the creator, set the stage.
And then, with others, you create.
You create your reality, as in:
I am the creator and I am responsible.

YOU ARE THE INITIATOR

Attesting to a change is different
than accepting the change.
Attesting is saying, yes, there is a change.
Approving it for you, is accepting it for yourself.

If you create something
that you do not want to accept,
then how is it that you cannot
change it right away?

Well, it works this way:
the change took time to implement,
and by not liking it
you are asking for a new change,
and this is another time element.

It is an aberration
in that you need to have a new thought,
which in the future
implements the change to the change.

Change is good. At least, that is what they say.
Well, yes, however, in a way,
changes are not made by them,
as you are the initiator of the changes
falling on you.

CHANGE IS GOOD

Change is good when it is requested
and comes out as you suggested.
However, if the message is not clear,
then what is it you glean?

You get a mumble jumble
that you need to unravel.
Therefore, you ask for another change,
and this will set you back
in achieving that
which you have asked for before.

If you don't like your moment,
change it in the present,
and then the future
will stem from your now.

Does this require an analysis?
Not really, as living from day to day
should be judged by a satisfaction factor,
not by some intellectual reasoning.

Change your circumstances not by asking,
but by living what you want.
Live in the present to make it the best
and then the change of a change
will not be required.
Then the future will be stemming from the present
that is looked after moment by moment
in the now.

Change is good.
Think well and do not dwell
on that which is not to your liking.
Stop complaining and be always ready
to change what needs to change in the present,
then you will not come to resent
your future.

CHANGE TO FIND THE NEWNESS

Change is inevitable and is good.
Changing is a way of dissolving for yourself
the areas of the most concern.

Change and you will find the newness.
Change and you will find the goodness,
the goodness within you
and the goodness within others
that are seeking just like you
to discover the truth about themselves.

Your growth is a spiritual need.
Therefore, you need to be clear
that your growth can be accomplished
anywhere.

ALLOW YOURSELF TO BECOME YOU

Be ready to live the consequences
if you don't release your stresses.
Be ready to live the consequences
if you don't learn to pace yourself.
Be ready to live the consequences
if you will not allow yourself
to become you.

You are you, and that is what you need to follow.
You are a person that is not hollow.
You are a person who is engaged in a search.
You are a thought identity, and, the best,
you will be rewarded for your search.

You will understand who you are
through your senses
that are being developed today.
These senses are a gate
to the consciousness that is vast,
so vast, that you can cast your fishing rod
and never reach the bottom.

CHANGE IS INEVITABLE

Change is inevitable and is not to be postponed,
you can no longer linger.
But then, why not?
You have been lingering before.

So, the change. Change is inevitable,
you don't need to fear it.
Change will always appear when you need it.
You changed yourself many times.
Every change is good and is welcome.

Change to come back to your spiritual senses.
Change to come back
to your absolute understanding of yourself.
Change to come back and smell the roses.
Change to understand who you are.

Changes stem from an atmospheric pressure,
from a changed environment,
from changed needs,
from realization of wants,
from your efforts,
from many, many reasons.

Only change that is good
is the change initiated by you.
What does it mean?
Well, let's come out clean,
you are a creator, remember?

If someone tries to change you for their sake
that is not going to help,
and the change will be futile,
as it is not seeded within.

You cannot be helped
if you don't help yourself.
You cannot be helped
if you don't count on yourself.
You cannot be helped
if you don't stand up and say,
this is my way and I will do it as I see it.

The power to change comes from within.
The decisions are yours.

YOUR INNER SELF NEEDS A CHANGE

It is not an easy task
to clean up your house
after centuries of abuse
when you misused
the laws of the Universe.

All is remembered. All is written in time.
It is a part of your akashic records.
It is looked up from time to time
to see the progress, to check the virtues,
to manage the outcome, to measure.

To measure the performance, you say?

Oh well, perhaps it can be called that way.
It is mostly a performance as measured by you.
You are not checked, you are not classified
to be good or bad.

You are not checked,
you are the one who does the checking,
as you are the one who wants to develop yourself,
as you are your own student,
teacher and prophet.

Things are sometimes in flux,
sometimes they are changing.
Change may come
when it is requested from outside,
however, the most important change
is the one requested from inside.

Your inner self needs a change,
and it makes sure that it happens
via pleasant or unpleasant experiences.
This scenario is not just assigned to you,
all are going through similar circumstances.

The "change" scenario asks for the following:
perception, recognition of the nudging to change,
a will and discipline to proceed,
a will and discipline to continue.
It asks for the checkpoints to say,
yes, I achieved this, and I need to go on
with this and this and that.

What are your checkpoints?
Is it your satisfaction level?
Is it your happiness and joy?
It is all the above and more.
It is you, who is the most important of all.
If you are not satisfied, nobody is.

FACILITATE THE CHANGE

You must orient yourself.
What is true? Is it you and your world,
or is it us and our world?
It is such that we don't know,
as all the things are on the move,
all is sparkling, changing, daring,
all is craving, doing, praying.

Alas, nothing is written in stone.
Alas, you are the one
who can take you home.
Nobody else will do it for you,
as nobody else is that which is you.
Nobody is in tune with you.
Nobody can translate
what is bothering you.

You are the one
who wants things to be changed.
You are the one who pines for an exchange
of ideas between the worlds,
of messages that will feel like a rose,
of things that float between spaces
that are transparent to regular folks.

The folks who are asleep for centuries to come,
as they are not the ones to comment on:
Oh yes, look at the sky. Who lives there?
Oh yes, look at that far reaching outlet of energy
that is spiralling away from that point that is me,
as I am connected with all and my Thee.

CHART YOUR OWN ROUTE

So there, our dear, do you understand?
You, only you, can facilitate the change,
and the change is within, not without.

It does not matter who you are,
if you are a king or a pauper,
you will be judged.

But you are your own judge.
You are your own maker
who charts her own route,
and you are the one who makes sure
that your charted map is right.

We know, it can be hard,
as you are not immune to influences from without.
But do as we say, control your thoughts,
as these are vehicles that created your past
and they create your today and future,
as you are marching toward us.

CLARITY

CLARITY IS REQUIRED

Sameness is not required.
You can have your own thoughts and sights,
and you will.
However, clarity counts and can only happen
if you are clear yourself, clear.

Otherwise, when you are not clear
you are reeling from influences
about who you are,
where you are going,
and where you will end.

Conquer yourself
by clearly expressing yourself.
Be clear.
Formulate a clear thought
and administer that to yourself.

It is not for you to solve others' vices.
It is not for you to solve others' problems.
It is for you to clarify your concepts.
It is for you to clearly define your own objects
and let others live their experiences.

When you are clear,
your clarity enables others' clarity.
Your clear speech and thought helps others
to understand what needs to happen,
to bring the solutions by themselves
to themselves.

You can vitally affect others by knowing
when you, as a spiritual being,
are clear and in command of your destiny.

MASTERING THE MIND

Have the end result in your mind,
then state it
and wait for the Universe to provide.

The Universe will obediently deliver
what is requested by you.
The Universe will obediently say,
my master, have a good day,
here are your requests delivered on time.

Hmm, you say, this is really neat.
So, I don't have to lift a finger?
How quaint, I like that!

Oh no, no, do not take it like that.
The right thought sets the action in the motion,
and by continuous right thought
you will get what you want.

So, what does it mean?

Be clear in your thoughts.
Say who you are.
State the purpose and what you want.
Have an end product in your mind.
Repeat it several times.

Wait for the Universe to deliver what you want.
Thank the Universe for what you've got,
as if it has been already delivered.

Behave as if all is an existing state.
And then, that state of your mind
becomes a state of the physical fact,
and your wish becomes a reality.

Clarity is the beginning. Be clear.
Do not say I do not like what I have,
Universe, make a change for me.
You tell the Universe what it needs to be
then proceed thanking and believing in it.
Set the stage, and the result will come.
Let the result happen by setting your condition.

This is called mastering your mind.
Do not, repeat, do not leave your mind
running the scenarios.
Do not allow your mind
to take over and chatter endlessly.
Do not allow your mind to run away
and you appear to be without a thought
endlessly involved in your own chattering mind.

Do not allow yourself to be immersed in scenarios,
state clearly what you want!

BE CLEAR, FREE AND HAPPY

You need to clarify your position to yourself.
You need to observe yourself
to decide who you are
and then apply the thoughts to yourself in a way
that you want to create your day.

Your ways are your ways to live
and they will not be, to your chagrin,
always the ways you were hoping for.
Create consciously and willingly,
and then it will be interpreted knowingly
by the gods.

Be clear about what you think and do.
Be clear about what you ask for.
Be constantly scrutinizing your goal.
State it clearly and appropriately,
as an unclear statement
may not be what you mean,
as this will misinterpret your will
and then the action
will not follow in the right interaction
between the gods and yourself.

Universe is here, beside you,
and is expecting you
to take the reins and prepare yourself
to be clear, free and happy.

CLEARLY DESIRE

What does it mean to create?
If you imagine that you create something new,
know that all exists and has been for millennia.

What you do by creating is uncovering.
You are uncovering the truths
that are here but are not clear.
You, by creating, are uncovering
that the new is old. And it may be
that it has been already told,
but it needs to be told again and again
in a completely new, unique way.

Forget all your troubles.
Feel that life is full of bubbles
of joy and unfolding pleasures
that are coming to you,
if you open yourself to those feelings
and do not dwell on the reality
that you created previously
by thoughts that were not coherent,
that were cloudy, that were pessimistic,
that were not too optimistic.

I am sure you are getting our drift.
I am sure that you know that this gift,
the gift of creation from the spiritual world,
from the place that is of an untold,
untold beauty, of creative powers,
of knowledge, is yours,
if that is what you clearly desire.

Notice the world clearly, as that is the clue.
Clearly is the word, and we have been told
by you and others that the word clear
is not too easy to comprehend,
as it is a word that is not expressed
the best by most of you
who are on Earth.

This is not a complaint or discouragement.
This is a way to say
that if you understand that creation is the way,
the way to live,
to win all your battles,
then you will understand that the matter
is pliable by thought
and is not, repeat, is not, given,
as it is your thought that creates your lot.

DESIRE TO BE SO

Matter is pliable. It is flexible.
It is what results from a thought.
Matter is not pliable to those who cannot
understand what pliable means.

You are the one who creates,
who makes the reality stick
and come to the surface
after the thoughts have sprouted
and breached the pond of concealment
to the point of a physical object
becoming visible to your eyes.

Demand the best of yourself
and you receive the best.
Demand the worst of yourself
and you receive the worst.
You can do anything,
as long as you desire one thing—
desire it to be so.

Desire it with desire that is clear as can be,
with desire that is yours and not theirs.
Desire it with desire that is clearly defined,
as you cannot desire if you are without
clear understanding of what you want.
Desire. Desire that is clear.

CLARITY

Nothing comes out from despair
but a lot can be had
from a clear, excited head.

Clear your head.
Clear your head of pollution,
of indictments, of accusations,
of minimalistic thoughts,
of burgeoning hate.

An analytical mind is of no help,
as it is constantly turning all over
to find a thread that it could unravel.

So, what is it that is required?
What is the best of all?

It is a clear head that is listening.
Listening to your calling.
Listening to your intuition.
Listening to your pressing issues.
Listening to all that is trying
to burst to the surface.

Have your mind clear.
A muddy mind is not effective.
A muddy mind is a hindrance.
A muddy mind is a burden.

YOU MUST UNDERSTAND

It is not what it seems, or is it?
All is not what it is, or is it?
All is not going to happen
as you think it should, or will it?

All is what you perceive.

If you perceive you are not welcome,
you will not be.
If you perceive you are not a part of something,
you will not be.
If your perceive that you are neglected,
then you will be.

Be yourself in understanding of yourself.
Be positively involved
with creating your own Universe
that is pliable to your wishes,
your wants and your taste.

If you want out, say, I am out.
Do not say I am in, and then wonder
from circumstances that are available
which lesser evil you will choose.

You are out, so be it.
You are in, so be it.
Do not be lukewarm about anything,
as nothing then happens.

You must understand
the consequences of procrastination.
You must understand the consequences
of an opinion that is negative.
You must understand what you are worth,
and you are worth a lot.

BE CLEAR IN WHAT YOU WANT

You must understand
that worth is not measured in money
but it is measured in your character,
the way you deal with situations,
the way you deal with people,
the way you deal with anomalies
or what you yourself perceive as an anomaly.

Substitute what you want to happen—
if you want to be a queen be a queen,
do not be a pauper.
If you want to be a pauper,
do not pretend you are a queen.

But, you may say,
I don't know what I want to be.
And that is the first big mistake
to be lingering in saying such a thing.

Do not procrastinate.
Decide and act.
Surrender to circumstances.
Be open-minded to your wants.
Be open-minded to the situations
and to the people you encounter
throughout the events of your life.

Remember, all is well if you think so
and it is not if you don't.
This does not mean to cover
what you don't like.

Just simply state:
I am out; I wasn't in on my terms.
I want out, an easy comfortable way.

BE DILIGENT IN STEPWISE SPECIFICATION

Be diligently detailed and all will work out.
Do not leave any ground uncovered.
Be diligent in stepwise specification
of what you desire.

For instance, you can write.
Cannot you write? Yes, you can.
So say, I can write and I will.
And you will.

Then say, I will sell what I write.
Then you will.
Say, people will like what I write
and they will buy. And so on.

Do you see the pattern?
You are what you create by your thought,
and you are the one to apologize
to yourself if you are not.

Let it be known what your choice is
and then circumstances will transpire
to support your choice.

INTUITION

FEELING OF KNOWINGNESS

Arrest your thoughts,
arrest your mind.
Flow of intuition is here
to guide you from within,
not from the outside.

It is here to guide you.
It is here to amend you.
It is here to explain.
It is here not to complain.
It is here. It is your guide,
and it is you, in your own heart,
who is listening to that intuition.

Intuition is a feeling of knowing
when you don't.
Intuition is a feeling of knowing
things that are buried,
that are here and are not seen,
that are, but links are severed,
that are, but are not preserved.
It is that knowledge within,
within you.

INTUITION IS A CLEAR SIGN

When you listen to that
which is within you,
be careful to understand.
Is this my ego thought
or is it a finer insight?

If it feels icky or you are not sure,
be wise not to endure
the consequences of that thought,
as that is not,
that is not intuition.

Intuition is a clear insight.
Intuition is a clear sign
of things to come.
Intuition is a message from God
that is within.

You are intuitively tuning in to the world
of the music of higher spheres,
of Universal love and eternal bliss,
of medieval, of old and new rules,
that are Universal laws.

Intuition...

INTUITION IS THE WAY TO LIVE

Melodrama is when we say,
I cannot take it anymore
and I will jump off the bridge
and then nothing will bother me anymore.

After this outburst people quiet down,
as the thorn is out and they are done
until the next occasion when they say,
oh yes, I've had enough
and I am going to jump off the bridge again.

Hmm, hmm, what are we saying?
We are saying, do not jump
but keep your head on.
Listen well to your intuition.
Listen well to your heart
and you always will be smart,
and you will glean from yourself.

Intuition is the way to live,
otherwise, you encounter lots of grief.
Grief that is not needed if you follow what is said,
as it is for you to understand,
to understand and follow your intuition.

Intuition is the mother of invention.
It is a way to comprehend your Self,
that part of yourself which is not of this Earth,
which is waiting to help you and tell
about the world you can have,
if you just listen to your intuition.

IMAGINATION

LEARN HOW TO IMAGINE

Imagining is a tool
that helps one to concoct a theory.
Learn how to imagine.
Learn to be with that feeling
of imagining.

Imagining is a technique
when you see without eyes,
you hear without ears,
you speak without words.

Imagining is a gift of God.
Imagining is a way of transporting yourself
to where you normally would not be.
It is a way of doing
what you normally would not do.

Imagining clears passages of time and space.
Imagining says, oh yes, oh yes,
I can be that, I can do that.
I can become what I desire to be.

Imagine and see yourself the way you want,
and then enjoy the fruits of your imagination.

YOU ARE MULTIDIMENSIONAL

You, yourself, show the way to yourself.
An appropriate learning period is required
until the pupil is ready to graduate.

You can conquer yourself
by changing your attitudes,
by changing your ways of interfacing
with yourself and with others
in such a way
that you will envision your success.

You will envision you enlarging yourself
to the point that you will understand
that your reality is multidimensional
and it is not of the kind
you can see and feel with the five senses,
but you view and hear
with your omnipotent eyes,
with your omnipotent ears.

CLOSE YOUR EYES AND IMAGINE

You cannot comprehend
everything all at once.
However, the time is ripe
for you to graduate.

To graduate from a little girl
and become a woman of wisdom.
From a little girl to a person
who is entitled to sight
that is invisible to earthly eyes,
and sound that is unheard by earthly ears.

Close your eyes and imagine
a world of immense beauty.
Close your eyes and imagine
a world of unknown colours.

Close your eyes and comprehend
that your earthly eyes
can only see what they see,
but they cannot go beyond seeing
behind the curtain of three-dimensional reality.
They cannot help you to open the curtain
that is covering the magnificent view.

RESPONSIBILITY

DESTINED TO COME TO A CONCLUSION

All is destined to come to a conclusion.
All is destined to arrive.
Know that if you do not arrive today,
you will arrive tomorrow.

Your sojourn on Earth is nearing the end,
but you need to comprehend
that it is not finished yet.

To finish your travels it is required
to love yourself, to love your kind,
to love all around,
to be honest, truthful,
to not be afraid of being yourself,
to allow yourself
to follow your dreams
and your wants.

Being yourself
is the best gift to your Self,
being one who cares and dares,
being one who takes into account
humanity and oneself.

Do not waste another lifetime.
Move ahead! Move ahead with your dreams.
You are destined to go to places,
places of your own,
traveling through your large mind,
seeing through your large eyes,
listening through your large ears.

With the right beliefs all is well
and your planned progress will prevail,
as all is destined to come to a conclusion,
all is destined to arrive.

RESPONSIBLE FOR YOUR THOUGHTS

The Universe is responsible for results.
You are responsible for your proper thoughts,
and your thoughts need to say:

I am who I am. I am a responsible person
who is responsible for my own destiny.
These are my wants,
please Universe bring them to me.
Thank you Universe for listening,
and thank you for the results.

Be specific. Be bold.
Be certain that the results will be delivered.
This prepares the soil and the seed will sprout,
and you will have what you want.

You can reach milestones when you do not gripe,
when you positively identify your joys,
when in all situations you see good.
If you think of bad, it will be raised
and propagated again.

Honesty to yourself is a virtue to possess.
Be a creature who is firm to express
thoughts that are easy to comprehend,
to assure that right thoughts start
to proliferate toward the Universe.

The Universe fulfills your thoughts
and then you can make room for a new want
that will also be fulfilled.

This is not greed,
as when no wants are present
the development is held up.
It is slow, it is delayed.

All is well. The bell, the bell,
listen to the bell, to the sirens
that are announcing that it is time,
time to affirm the above.

TO BE OR NOT TO BE

To be or not to be is getting clearer.
To be or not to be.
To be is one,
and not to be is another reality.

You are the one to conquer your fears.
You are the one to experience your bliss.
You are a dream that comes through.
You are a river that flows through,
you are the one who falls through.

Through the abyss of unconsciousness.
Through the abyss of not knowing
when to stop your own being
falling through the abyss,
the abyss of reincarnations.

Your intrepid, absolute,
masculine and feminine body,
is changing into somebody
every time you incarnate.

Your incarnations are a stream of events
that are taking you from place to place,
that are willingly or unwillingly,
wittingly or unwittingly,
consciously or unconsciously,
taking you for a ride.

Stop being taken.
Stop being pushed and prodded.

Do your own pulling,
your own meticulous planning
to arrive at the destination of your choice,
of your own doing, of your own.

Do not sit and wait for things to come,
but be the one who is ready
to create your new you.

BE A DRIVER

Be a driver as you were meant to be.
You can become a driver, you can.
You can change your fate.
You can turn right or left.
You can ride where you want.
You can abruptly finish what you don't want.
You can sit and ponder,
you can do anything.

Hmm, now you wonder.
What is it I can do and how?
How do I do it now?

Listen to your heart.
If it says stop, stop.
If it says go, go.
If it says no, then no.
If it says yes, then yes.
Elementary Watson?
Hmm, yes and no.

First you must know
which voice is your heart's,
and which voice is the one
that takes you away
from your prime,
from your path.

Listen to your inner advice.
Listen to your inner calling.
Listen to your inner voice.

Listen to your absolutely convincing
inner urge to discover your roots,
to discover your origins.

BANAL IT AIN'T

Banal it may seem, banal it may be.
Banal it may feel, but it is not.

Banal is not your wish.
Banal is not your feeling of loneliness,
your feeling of being forgotten,
your feeling of looking and searching
for that eternal happiness.

Your happiness, as it is within,
must be recognized.

Examine your every whim. Why do I feel like that?
Examine your thrust. Why am I pulled that way?
Examine your values. Do I do what I really want?
Do I listen to others first, then to me?
Do I ponder on events that are not mine,
that belong to those around me,
that are their actions and facts?

If that's what it is, break that habit.
Break away from it, break away.
Break away, do as we say.

Through meditation, your freedom will surface.
Your mental powers will hone onto what matters—
what matters for you, what presents you
with your choices, with your own events,
with your own tasks,
with your own molasses of life.

Spirit is here to embrace you.
Spirit is here to offer an understanding,
to offer you peace and quiet,
to offer you emotional support,
to offer you your own world,
where your life will unfold,
where your story is told,
where your own maturity comes along,
where your own, very own Source comes
and offers you her support.

Where your very own ideas
bring you enlightenment,
where your very own world will happen
and will bring you along
for a ride that is programmed to your song,
that is a life of reason of not committing treason,
treason to your ideas.

ALLOW YOURSELF

Allow yourself to flourish.
Allow yourself to invite the inevitable,
the inevitable that is only seemingly that.

Once with you, it will change
to inviting and warm and wanted,
to pleasant and true
and counted.

Counted as an experience that is a must,
as it is leading you toward
your truth of being God.

Allow yourself the highest self-esteem.
Allow yourself the highest kind of happiness.
Allow yourself then expect it to happen.

Allow yourself to experience your beliefs,
and then to change them.
Allow yourself to speak freely.

Allow yourself to view things
from a different perspective.
Allow yourself to cry when necessary.
Allow yourself to leave, if you feel like leaving.

Allow yourself to quench your quest for the truth.
Allow yourself to experience God.
Allow yourself to change your habits.
Allow yourself to dream and risk.

Allow yourself to bless yourself.
Allow yourself to be yourself.
Allow yourself to be, just be.
Allow yourself.

A CANVAS OF LIFE

Best of all is to come.
Best of all is almost done.
Best of all is very near,
and let's make it clear—
it is not easy to understand
that best of all is always here.

It is as the situation needs.
It is as the calling is
calling for justice, as seen
from above, not from below.

The best of all is always here.
And, our dear,
the best of all is yet to come,
as it is a mirror of things that are done,
as it is a pool of ideas
that was in place for some time.

So, what is the best of all today?
Waiting? Drooling for something to come?
Dreading something to come?
Or is it a life that is a smooth ride?

It is a mishmash of all, as it is a painting of all
that needs to be painted on a canvas of life.

A canvas of life is large.
It is quite huge. There are possibilities of deluge,
and any given possibility involves others.

99

The result, when the canvas is painted,
cannot be predicted.
It cannot be predicted to the tee,
as there are many, many choices given.

And therefore you,
the maker of your destiny,
are responsible for your own canvas,
are responsible for the outcome.
We cannot predict it,
we can only see the main line.

Play, play, play.
Do not be so serious, do not be so intent.
Play, play, play. This is your own play.
You are the main character on display
of your own stage, of your own game
that is your own life story.

Your life story is a story of courage and cowardice.
It is a story of mundane and heroic,
of sweet and sour, of perplexing and clear,
of foolish and wise, of everything far and near,
of all contrasts, joys and happiness.

A canvas of life is quite large.
Create your best canvas.

RESPONSIBILITY STARTS WITH YOU

Negligence, responsibility, annoyance—
all are a part of living, all are a part of growing.

The truth is not one, there are many.
And with the probabilities chosen,
responsibility is changing.

The advice from here is:
do not frivolously admire yourself.
Do not frivolously blame others.

Be in love with all your sisters and brothers
through being in love with yourself first.
By satisfying you, you will be taken care of,
and then others will follow the plot.

Responsibility is a way of saying:

I will do the best for myself
without hurting others.
I will do the best for myself
without forgetting others.
I will do the best for myself
by being who I am.
I will do the best for myself
by admitting that I am who I am.
I am concerned about the care I am giving.
I am thoughtful, I am in charge.
I am strong and invincible.
I am.

Responsibility starts with you.
Responsibility is a way of telling you
that you can have what you want.
All you need to do is to listen to your heart
that tells you who you are.

Let bygones be bygones.
Let bygones be really gone.
You are the only one who is important.
Take care of you.
Be joyful.
Be thoughtful.

IT IS NOT ABOUT A PLACE IN SOCIETY

Responsibility is, as understood by you,
a way to perceive yourself in society.
You judge yourself on how you attach
yourself to the responsibility.

You believe that responsibility
gives you a place to interface
with those around you.

Responsibility is not about a place in society.
Responsibility is about a relationship
with yourself, with you.

If you are responsible to you
then you know who you are.
If you are responsible to others
then you belong to their scale of judging.

Of course, you can be responsible to both,
and then at most, you will have both worlds.

However, primary responsibility is with you.
You are responsible to yourself.
It is when you say, I will do this my way
and I will achieve the results.

Then you know what needs to be done.
Otherwise, "they" will be talking about a plan
on how to achieve the results
you are expected to provide.

UNDERSTAND WHO YOU ARE

All, definitely all, is depending on you.
Your decisions influence you and others.
Your decisions are known to the Universes.
Your decisions are known to gods.
Your decisions are all up to you,
not up to us.

Your reality is created
as your thoughts congeal the etheric mass
into objects you call matter.
To create takes you a while,
longer, than to make someone smile.

You do not comprehend how you do it.
It is not known and it is hidden
within the reality of the things
that you perceive as new,
when you see them anew.

The reality that is being created
is not easily understood by you,
as it is difficult to see how it becomes.
It is difficult to see how it happens,
as it comes
from invisible.

The reality, which is in the making,
exists in the realm of thought.
That is how it exhibits itself,
that is how it comes to life,
through your imagination and your thought.

You have been enthralled into believing
that what you see is the real thing.
But the real thing you see
is a thing of the past,
as you, in your past, thought of that,
and now you live that reality.

You, as a creator, have a responsibility
to understand that you, solely you,
create that which is your bliss
and also that which can go amiss.

And amiss it goes,
as you do not fully understand
the powers you have.

You are a powerful being
that adjusts life to his wants.
You are a powerful being
who is steeped in the reality
of saints and gods.

BE ACCOUNTABLE TO YOURSELF

Be progressively more and more aware
of the waste you produce.
Be accountable to yourself.
Be decisively proactive,
be conservative with your time.

Is this contrary to what we teach?
Is it saying you cannot reach for the stars?
Oh no, this is not so.
You can reach, and are welcome to reach.
You can reach and you will not breach
anything we said before.

You can. And at the same time
be disciplined about your daily life.
You can be one to achieve what you want,
if you do not allow yourself to waste your time.

Be accountable to yourself.
Do not dilly-dally, be prompt.
Be open and honest about
what you can do
and what you cannot.

If you are accountable to yourself,
you will see the results soon.
You will see the results always,
not only once in a blue moon.

The world is yours to have,
reach for the stars

and be accountable to yourself.
If you do, and all do the same,
you will be accountable en masse.

Then great things will happen to humanity.
You will be in touch with the stars.
You will understand en masse who you are.
You will understand your future and your past.
You will be ready to incarnate or not,
depending on your wishes and wants.

TAKE THE REINS INTO YOUR OWN HANDS

The world is crumbling, the world of decay,
that at times seems nothing but prey,
where the rich are preying on the poor,
where you are at the mercy
of your own leniency,
as you are too lenient towards yourselves
and are not at the mercy of others.

You all need to understand here and now
that you, only you,
are the creators of your own realities.
You, only you, are your own bosses
and are responsible for scrutinizing your beliefs.

Responsibility starts
with responsibility for yourselves.
Take a responsible approach
and all will fall into place
and no gods and goddesses can change
the course you chart out for yourself.

Be responsible to yourself
and take the reins into your own hands!

STAND ON YOUR OWN TWO FEET

You act responsibly
when you respond to your needs,
when your needs are in synch
with the needs of others,
when all of you are in synch.

Responsibility is given to you
to be borne by you.
Your responsibility is to get rid
of every thorn you amass
throughout your journeys,
throughout your incarnations.

You incarnated many, many times.
You are within your own recycling class
of teaching and learning from yourself.
You are your own teacher.
You are your own maker
of your own Universe.

The responsible being is the one
who is standing on her own two feet.
Who is not depending on others.
Who is always thoughtful
of her sisters and brothers.

Who is always aware
that responsibility is hers,
that responsibility is everlasting joy
and is not a ploy to burden,
but to enlighten.

A GIFT OF SELF

Meticulously integrate
new ways into your schedule.
Discipline yourself to perceive
yourself as a maker, not a taker.
Do be insistent on getting your own timeframe.
Do find time to pursue the interests of yours
and of the Universal plane.

Capable management of your time
is of the utmost importance.
Regardless of how busy you are
you need to persevere in finding time
to contact your God,
to contact your Higher Self.

Your gift of Self
is the most important part of your life
you cannot evolve without.
Otherwise, you will not evolve as you could,
you will not speak your truth,
you will not bring yourself to your new state,
you will not be amongst those
who are in tune with the Universe.

You are a perceptive person
who is groomed to become
the master of herself.

Who is grooming you?
Who is attending to you?
Of course, it is you, of course.

Those, really those,
are the answers you already know.

You know all the truths.
You knew and know them now.
They are resurfacing here and there.
They are embedded in your consciousness.
They are the truths that never change.
They are ruling all in the Universe.

THE BEST THAT CAN HAPPEN TO YOU

You can resolve opening the gate,
the gate that lets the flood in,
the flood of consciousness
from within.

The gate is closed until you amass powers
to control that flood,
as the flood can smite you if you do not abide
the Universal laws.

The flood is only of help
if your yelp for help congeals into a power,
which can control that flood.

Flooding of consciousness
is a raw mystical way of understanding the ways
of creating your own reality,
of beckoning good-bye to duality,
of saying hello to oneness,
of saying welcome to your true Self.

Listen to your heart, to your feelings
that are abandoning your fears,
that are inviting a certainty of knowing
that you, as a godly being,
are in charge.

You are in charge, do you hear?
You are in charge.
Without a fear, step out and reach
to bring freedom to yourself,

to bring freedom of thought,
of creativity, of abandoned joy,
of absolute power over your destiny.
Bestow it on yourself freely.

Fear is out. Love is in.
Bestow it upon yourself my dear.
Bestow it upon others,
your sisters and brothers.

Best of all is to come and is here!
Let's make it clear, you, our dear,
are the best that can happen to you.

You may say,
how is it, how does it work?
Well, how can anything be better
for you than you?
How can anything different from you
be better for you than you,
than your own thoughts and wants?

THE APPRECIATION GIVEN TO YOU

Do not cover your responsibility
by thinking that you are not responsible.
Do not accept that you are the one
who is devoid of responsibility,
that you are the one
who is mercilessly involved with a living
that is not going anywhere.

Do find what life is all about.
Be of the view
that your reality is created by you.

And so it is. It is you, who creates herself.
It is you, who is mastering the stage,
the stage of endless changes
that take you back to your home.

You are responsible for happenings around you.
You are responsible for appreciation given to you.
And, as you appreciate yourself first,
then others appreciate you next.

Accountable, responsible.
To yourself, not to others.
Be accountable and responsible to yourself
and then automatically the rest is covered.

It is not the other way around.
First is you, then the rest
will fall into place.

ABUNDANCE

ABUNDANCE IS THE LAW

More is not the way to conquer yourself.
More is not the way to receive blessings.
More is a curse if taken to extreme,
more cannot be the law.
Abundance is, but it does not imply more.
Abundance is the law.

The law of the Universe is abundance for all,
therefore, you don't have to worry about more.
If all are blessed at all times, one cannot suffer.
If none is in need, the law is understood.
Love is a law, so is abundance.

The Universe is ready to give, just ask.
The Universe is ready to supply.
The Universe is ready, just apply.
Apply your thoughts
to follow the path of the Universal law
of abundance and love.

BE A PROUD CITIZEN OF THE EARTH

Some believe in poverty,
instead of the law of abundance and love.
To them, poverty means that it leads
toward an enlightenment
that it is a virtue of the Soul.

Is that what you believe?
Is that how you live?
Poverty is not the way to go.
Do respect abundance, love and joy.

Poverty of relationships, poverty of thoughts,
poverty of material substance.
None of this is a virtue,
none of this is a law.
All of this makes you crawl,
it makes you beg and crawl.

Do not beg. Be proud.
Be a proud citizen of the Earth.
Be proud and do not be a pauper.
Be proud to receive and keep
the blessing of the Universe—
abundance and love.

UNIVERSE IS ABUNDANT

Greed longs for more,
more power, more money,
more food, more, more.

Do not listen to any greed,
to greedy thoughts
of having more and more.
Do not listen to those,
as greed is the downfall
of humanity.

Greed is obeying your primitive,
very primitive urges of fear.
Fear of not having enough
when the Universe is abundant.
Fear of not having,
when others can.

Fears like those are stifling.
Fears like those can hurt.
Fear like those will unravel
your psyche to the point
that it is not, is not at all
listening.

Listening to ideas from the Universe,
listening to intuition,
listening to all throbbing, vibrating,
bobbing, squirming primordial mass
that you are a part off.

Primordial mass that is a given.
Primordial mass that is a soup,
soup of thoughts, ideas, intuition,
of revelations.

I WILL NOT WAIT, I WILL ACT

Deliver all worries to your gods.
Deliver all the requirements.
Deliver all sensible and foolish issues,
deliver details, as many as needed.

You are in a learning mode.
You are also in a prosperity lock
and you are not moving forward,
as you are waiting for something to come around.

Say:
I will not wait, I will act.
I do understand that I am the one
who is able to create, who can,
and will not wait for others to open the gate
to prosperity that has been eluding me,
that has been elusive.

MONEY IS ENERGY

Money is not evil,
money is energy.
Money is a divine power
to empower yourself.

Money is a gift from God.
Money is a way to be abundant
and independent,
to be always sufficient,
to be at peace with yourself.

Money is a blessing.
Money is a curse.
That depends only on you,
on your interpretation of the events
that surround money and you.

Best of all, money is everywhere.
Money is a substance of abundance—
abundance that is all around us,
as energy is free flowing
and is yours to have.

Money is for you to have and enjoy,
is for you to amass or to lose.
Your interpretation becomes your reality.
All is your thoughts that congeal into a lot
with which you then need
to deal with.

Enjoy the money and have no fright,
there is always a lot of it,
there is always abundance.
Enjoy life. Get what you might
when you feel joyful and free.

I AM RICH

Here is a thought.
Tonight, before you go to sleep,
please recite,
and don't think it is greed,
recite:

"I am rich, I am richly endowed.
I am immensely rich
in all that surrounds me.
I am rich, I am rich.
I am enjoying this."

We will tell all about the riches
that are free for all,
free, if you understand the law.
The law says there is abundance.

There is a lot and more
if you think there is.
It all depends on your thought.
Why don't you think riches
instead of scarcity?
Why don't you think riches
all the time?

DRUDGERY IS UNNECESSARY

Drudgery is a state
when you are working very hard
and the results are minimal,
and results are not obvious,
when duration accomplishes nothing.

In drudgery, the spirit is suppressed
and the mind is numbed.
In drudgery, the spirit is not well,
it is not participating, it is calling for help.

Drudgery is not brought from outside.
It is a state of your mind,
as, in drudgery and all other such states,
the primary culprit is yourself.

It is drudgery if you don't feel
your heart is a part of what you do.
It is drudgery if you feel
that reality is bestowed upon you,
and you are not experiencing joy
from doing what you do.

Drudgery is a way
of enslaving yourself by tasks
that are not pleasant to your heart,
that are a part of the scheme
that keeps you enslaved.

Arduous work is not the way.
Arduous work represents

not knowing where you are going.
Therefore, you are working hard
to suppress the feeling of not knowing
what you want.

Drudgery exhausts the body
while making the mind foggy.
Drudgery is unnecessary,
as drudgery is a state
brought on you by yourself.

Become your own enlightened boss,
do not enslave yourself again.
Keep drudgery out.

RICHES

Riches are not plentiful
if you think that you do not deserve them.

Rich are those who can believe
that they are endowed with riches
for the times to come.
Rich are those who are sure
about their worth.

A rich person says, I have riches,
thank you God.
A rich person is not contemplating and debating
if the riches will come or not.
A rich person knows that they are theirs,
knows that riches are abundant.

Riches are not that plentiful
if you allow yourself to contemplate
whether you deserve them.

Think riches. Believe in them.
Think riches.
Think of the Universe as abundant.

ABUNDANCE IS THE WAY

Is money the object of your worry?
Don't you believe by now
that abundance is the way of the Universe?
Don't you believe by now
that abundance is here for all?

After all, and we said this many times,
abundance is the way.
Let's be assured of that,
as it is a fact, abundance
is the way of the Universe—
money is always sufficient.

Money is a state of mind
and if you don't have that,
that state of mind,
then you may not have money.

Money is energy
that is available to all.
To those who do not shy from having it,
to those who understand
that the Universe is abundant,
that it is calling you
to take from its riches
and use it all for you,
for you own good.

Money is energy.
Energy that is flowing freely,
energy that is available to all.

ABOUT THE AUTHOR

Helena Kalivoda is devoted to sharing "heavenly" messages that support readers in transforming their lives. Lives of peace and happiness are available to those who learn the power of creation through an open heart as encouraged by Helena's books.

AWAKEN! Spirit Is Calling, Helena's first book, contains powerful truths for each person's journey. These poignant teachings were downloaded from Helena's guides and angels. Be prepared for your "aha" moments when reading the book.

Her second book, *WAKE UP! Your Heart Is Calling*, leads readers to realize that all aspects of humanity, when denied pure love, are bound to eventually fail and cannot be healthy. This book connects to an online environment where you can access extended resources to help you apply the learned principles.

WAKE UP! Prosperity Is Calling, Helena's third book, outlines The Seven Principles to Living a Life of Prosperity. These principles will become your truth and experience once you use them and live them consistently.

Currently, Helena is working on a new series of *Purposeful Mind* books of poetry. This book, *Creation*, is the first book of this series.

Helena holds a BA in Economics and B.Sc. in Computer Science. She is a mother of three, living in Canada. In 1997, she left the corporate world to continue the writing she started in the early nineties.

Visit www.awakenbyhelena.ca for more information about Helena Kalivoda's books.

www.ingramcontent.com/pod-product-compliance
Lightning Source LLC
LaVergne TN
LVHW091153080426
835509LV00006B/668